Bedtime Stories for Ages 2-6

12 Lovely Bedtime Stories for Children

Imogen Young

© Copyright 2021 - All rights reserved.

The content contained within this book may not be reproduced, duplicated or transmitted without direct written permission from the author or the publisher.
Under no circumstances will any blame or legal responsibility be held against the publisher, or author, for any damages, reparation, or monetary loss due to the information contained within this book. Either directly or indirectly.

Legal Notice:
This book is copyright protected. This book is only for personal use. You cannot amend, distribute, sell, use, quote or paraphrase any part, or the content within this book, without the consent of the author or publisher.

Disclaimer Notice:
Please note the information contained within this document is for educational and entertainment purposes only. All effort has been executed to present accurate, up to date, and reliable, complete information. No warranties of any kind are declared or implied. Readers acknowledge that the author is not engaging in the rendering of legal, financial, medical or professional advice. The content within this book has been derived from various sources. Please consult a licensed professional before attempting any techniques outlined in this book.

By reading this document, the reader agrees that under no circumstances is the author responsible for any losses, direct or indirect, which are incurred as a result of the use of information contained within this document, including, but not limited to, — errors, omissions, or inaccuracies.

Table of Contents

Ginny The Giraffe 6

Tom the Cat 22

The Story of The Little Marzipan Man 30

Stop Talking! 37

The Jaguar 45

Kendra the Kangaroo 52

Mother Duck 61

The Ox 66

Quin 77

The Red Fox 84

Noel the Newt Sings Too Loud 91

The Paper Airplane 97

Ginny The Giraffe

Ginny Giraffe has to go to bed at 8:00 at night. It's 7:00 right now and it's time to start getting ready for bed.

"Ginny?" Mother Giraffe called to Ginny. "It's 7:00 are you getting ready for bed?"

"Oh mom, do I have to? I am coloring in my new color book." Ginny responded

Ginny loved to color before bedtime. It helped her relax and calm down before bedtime.

"Yes dear, you have school tomorrow and you need to get some good sleep." Mother Giraffe responded

Ginny tried to act like she didn't hear her mother and she kept coloring. 30 minutes passed and Ginny was still coloring.

"Ginny?" Mother Giraffe called to Ginny. "It's 7:30 are you ready for bed?"

"Uh, I'm working on it mom," Ginny said trying to act like she was almost ready for bed

"Ginny, it's important that you get to bed on time. There is school tomorrow and you don't want to be too tired." Mother Giraffe tried to convince Ginny.

Ginny kept coloring and not following directions. Finally, her mother came into her room, "GINNY! What are you doing? Why are you not ready for bed?" Mother Giraffe questioned. Ginny looked up from her coloring book and shrugged her shoulders.

"I just want to keep coloring," Ginny said as she looked at her almost finished coloring page.

"You can finish it tomorrow young lady it's time to go to bed." Mother Giraffe instructed .

Ginny put the crayons of her at bay & closed her coloring book and also began getting all set for bed. She put on her preferred PJs, put the clothes of her in the unclean closets bin and headed to the bathroom. She washed the face of her and brushed the teeth of her. She surpassed by her mom 's room on the way of her back to the room of her.

"See mom I have ready for foundation and I still have five minutes to spare," Ginny stated proudly.

"Thank you, Ginny, you can color for 5 more minutes if you like but I want lights out at 8:00." Mother Giraffe said looking at Ginny seriously

Ginny ran to her room and took out her coloring things again. She lay on the floor and began to finish her picture. 10 minutes passed, 30 minutes passed and soon one hour had passed and Ginny was still coloring. She finished her picture and stood up to look at the time.

"Oh no, It's 9:00! I'm up way past my bedtime." Ginny said. She tiptoed to the bathroom one more time before bed but her Mother heard her.

"Ginny, are you still up?" Mother Giraffe called out from her bedroom

"Yes mom I'm sorry, I was coloring and I lost track on time," Ginny said hanging her head.

"You are likely to be tired in the early morning you have to drop by bed now." Mother Giraffe believed. Ginny hurried up and also went to bed.

Mother Giraffe came within at 7:00 within the early morning to wake up Ginny but Ginny was asleep extremely hard. Mother Giraffe was having a hard period waking her up.

"Ginny, Ginny you have to stand up and get prepared for school." Mother Giraffe begged.

Finally, Ginny got set up, got prepared and headed to college.

As Ginny sat in mathematics class, she started falling asleep. She kept attempting to remain awake though her eyes were quite heavy and also kept closing. She believed, "If I simply close the eyes of mine for a second, it will be okay and I will be able to pay attention to the teacher." Ginny closed the eyes of her for a minute or perhaps so she thought.

"Ginny?" Her teacher came to her desk. "Ginny do you think you're okay, you need to wake up today it is time to go home."

"Time going home? Did I rest through the entire day?" Ginny stated as she were around to the empty classroom

"Sadly, absolutely you did and it is time to go home today. You may try going to bed earlier." Her instructor suggested

Ginny gathered up the things of her and walked home from college. She walked in the home and her mom asked her the way her day was. Ginny Sighed as well as said, "I do not understand, I slept thru the entire day."

"I am not amazed, you had been up far too late." Mother Giraffe replied

Ginny headed up to the room of her. Because she slept all day at school, she'd a great deal of assignments to do.

"This isn't enjoyable. I want to color never do homework." Ginny stated to herself

Dinner time arrived, Ginny consumed and went right up to the room of her to eat her homework. 7:00

arrived and Ginny was nearly done with her schoolwork.

"Mom, I'm nearly done with the school work of mine. I will get all set for bed soon." Ginny informed the mother of her.

"Just view time Ginny, you do not wish to snooze thru the schooling working day again." Mother Giraffe reminded Ginny

7:30 rolled around as well as Ginny was completing the homework of her. She put all the books of her back into the book bag of her and then began getting all set for bed. She put on her preferred PJs, put the clothes of her in the unclean closets bin and headed to the bathroom. She washed the face of her and brushed the teeth of her. She surpassed by her mother 's space once more and also announced she was prepared for bed.

"Tonight I'm simply going going to sleep on time. I was way too exhausted now and I do not wish to sleep through class again and have a great deal of homework." Ginny was detailing "I needed to style though I'd a lot of school work."

"Get a little sleep. Tomorrow is a brand new day." Mother Giraffe motivated Ginny.

Ginny headed off to sleep and this was merely 7:50 she was going to sleep ten minutes earlier though she fell asleep instantly.

The morning arrived and mom giraffe arrived in, "Time to stand upwards Ginny." Mother Giraffe shook Ginny awake. Ginny Popped up great awake with a grin on her face.

"I had such a great sleep, mom. I am very happy I went to sleep on time." Ginny stated happily.

"Me too, Let us hop to it for ready to head to school." Mother Giraffe stated as she left the room.

Ginny got prepared and headed off to college. She sat in category with wide eyes and exhilaration that she was broad awake and prepared for the day. Halfway through the morning, the teacher announced the category was about to have has a surprise gathering before the saturday. Ginny was very glad she wasn't sleeping through class now so she can enjoy the party. The party was enjoyable, they played video games and consumed snacks most of the fun things you can imagine at a gathering. After school, Ginny rushed house to inform the mom of her about the party.

"I'm so happy you were awake for the bash today." Mother believed.

From that evening on Ginny made certain she viewed time and also stopped coloring in time that is enough getting prepared for bed. She went to bed promptly each night since she did not wish to be too tired for more surprise parties that the class of her might be having.

Herman Hermit Crab obtains Crabby He swings and hits the baseball and goes soaring way to the outfield. Herman Hermit crab scurries lowered by the starting line safe at first. He high fives the starting advisor and becomes ready to watch and see if he can steal 2nd base. The following batter gets up as well as becomes ready to hit the ball. Swish- Strike one

"Come on buddy!" yelled Herman "you can do it hit that ball."

The pitcher winds upwards as well as throws the ball. Herman begins to work and steal second base. The batter swings again-SWISH-Strike two. But Herman created it to second base. He started clapping the claws of his and cheering on the batter once again, "You can do it, hit me home!" Herman yells against second base.

Right here comes the pitch & Herman begins to take 3rd base…. "FOUL BALL." Shouts the referee on the home plate. Herman scowls and heads back again to second base.

Next two Pitches "BALL" yells the umpire.

Herman knew he could steal 3rd on this particular subsequent pitch therefore he crouched down as well as got all ready to bolt down the baseline. The Pitcher winds up and also allows the heel roar across the plate as well as Herman takes off. The catcher throws the heel but Herman slides in and it is safe.

"HaHa I just knew it," Herman said proudly "I knew I would make it," he tells the 3rd foundation advisor.

The count is currently 3 balls and two strikes; a complete count. Herman watches the pitcher and also examines the coach of his signal to steal the base or even wait. He gets the signal to wait. "Oh male, I can generate it," Herman mumbles under the breath of his. He turns to the coach of his, "Let me take home coach I can help make it, I understand I can."

"No wait right here Herman, I believe we can score whether he hits the heel, whether not we are going to wait for next batter." The advisor encouraged Herman to wait. Herman launched a grumpy face and then stood on 3rd base pouting type. The batter swung and also blooped it correctly down the third baseline. Herman was not focusing and he started to run. The 3rd base player picked up the heel tagged Herman and subsequently threw it first to get the batter out. A double play.

Herman stood currently there by way of a shocked appearance on his face. "Come on Herman allows go, we have to draw the field," the coach stated as he ran to the dugout.

Herman walked to the dugout unhappy. He grabbed the mitt of his and headed out with the industry. He walked out to center field dragging the feet of his and taking the time of his.

"Batter up!" yelled the umpire. Herman wasn't actually out to the position of his yet. He turned and scowled with the umpire as he made the way of his out to the outfield. Herman stood available like he was patiently waiting for a bus. He did not move when a heel was struck and he did not cheer on the team of his when they made a great play. Lastly, they have three outs & Herman's staff headed back again in to bat.

"What's the problem of yours, Herman?" Asked one of many players.

"Hello-I got out. Did not you view that?" Herman snapped having a crabby voice.

"We all leave sometimes; it is not a huge deal. When the coach sent you and you got out it is not the fault of yours you are doing what you were informed to do." Another participant chimed in.

"Well he DIDN'T mail me though I just knew I could make it," Herman grumbled.

Herman team made it throughout the batting order as well as Herman was as much as bat again. "Herman, you're up!" His mentor called out. Herman grabbed the bat of his and slumped the way of his to the batter package. Herman stood there watching for the best pitch. He just viewed as the pitcher pitched three attacks in a row. Herman was out. He dropped the bat of his and also grumbled to the bench.

"Hey, your crabby mindset isn't assisting the team." The ensuing batter stated as he travelled toward the plate.

"Whatever!" Herman snapped.

The inning was more than as well as Herman's team was taking the industry.

"Herman, I would like you to sit this particular inning out. We're a group and everybody has to participate to do well." His mentor stated.

Herman flopped bad on the bench and viewed as his staff fielded heel an made outs.

"Herman, you're a great player...but you are great," His mentor mentioned as they sat observing the various other players. "You have to become a leader even when things do not go as you wished. Your attitude impacts everyone. When you remain positive the team can be positive or in some point, they simply will not wish to play with you."

Herman sat, listened and also considered what the coach had stated though he was currently crabby about getting away. But what the mentor had said looked like a great stage. Even if Herman got out in case he might attempt to find out from the components on the game, he did not like he can figure out how to be a much better player and maybe teach other players challenging tricks to play much better.

"Can I remember to go again in coach?" Herman requested the next inning.

"I do not understand Herman, how's your attitude?" Coach questioned.

"I am prepared to do much better. I realize that if I'm crabby concerning what I did, it looks as I'm crabby about what everybody does and I did not mean for which to happen." Herman discussed.

When the staff had taken the field the next inning Herman ran out to the position of his and started becoming the staff player, he just knew he was. He was cheering on the staff which generated plays and also congratulated them once they made an out. Eventually all the other players started chiming in on the staff support. Herman stood within the outfield and felt proud that he might alter the attitude of his and never be so crabby.

He recognized that no matter if things do not go the way of yours you can decide how you can feel about it and deciding to check out the great things usually makes you feel happier.

Tom the Cat

Once in a time, there seemed to be a cat named Tom that lived in a town. 1 day he discovered a photograph of his good friend Milo who lived in the countryside. Upon seeing the picture, Tom thought it will be enjoyable to surprise him with a visit also he establish away to perform that.

After walking for hours, Tom reached Milo´s house:

- Hello, my dear friend. – said Tom, happily.

- How are you? – asked Milo, surprised to see him.

- I am doing well, thanks. I wanted to surprise you. – said Tom, happily.

- What a beautiful surprise. – said Milo – Welcome to the countryside. I am so glad you came from the city just to visit me. That is so kind of you.

The two little friends started talking about their lives:

- You have had such a long journey. You must be tired now. Why don't you go freshen up? In the meantime, I will prepare something delicious to eat. – said Milo, happily.

While Tom stayed at home to rest, Milo headed towards the farm to pick some vegetables. Meanwhile, Tom, wanting to shower, accidentally finished all the water:

- Ah, there is so little water. My city is much better. – said Tom, feeling annoyed

Tom came out feeling irritated.

- Come, we will eat outside. The weather is just lovely today and I have just prepared a ton of yummy things for you. – said Milo with a welcoming smile.

On the table, there were sweet potatoes, fresh beetroots, turnips and fresh milk. Milo took a plate a put a little bit of everything on it for Tom:

- Is that what you eat in the countryside? This food is bland. It's just tasteless. – said Tom

Milo tried very hard to impress his friend and make him happy, but unfortunately, he did not succeed. After lunch, Milo decided to go for a walk so he could show Tom around:

- Ah, the atmosphere is very new! I may also smell the fragrance of those gorgeous flowers. What is this green stuff? - requested Tom, strangely enough.

- Those're new peas. - replied Milo

While hiking, the 2 friends came across damp compost and Tom covered the nose of his with his hands: - What's this terrible smell? It's very dirty here. My city is very clean. Honestly, my dear good friend, I do not know how you can live here. I can never live here. Just how can you eat that food that is terrible? Just how can you live around bugs and all of this dirt? Come with me, I am going to take you to the beautiful town of mine so you'll forget about each this. - stated Tom.

- I'm sorry if you didn't like the foods, but there's absolutely nothing wrong with it and it's not bad to dwell in the countryside. Everything is fresh. and natural - replied Milo.

- I'd love you to include me with the city, just for a couple of days. I'd love showing you how I live. I am going to have you eat much more., nuts, pasta, and cheese - stated Tom, enthusiastically.

- That seems great! - replied Milo.

- I'm certain you are going to be delighted. - stated Tom.

Once they went to Milo's home, Tom began packing his bag: - It's currently period for me to keep. Thank you a lot for your welcoming. I'd a wonderful time. I am going to see you soon in my gorgeous town. - stated Tom.

Several days later, Milo crammed his bags to visit the friend of his in the city, as promised. After walking for time, Milo lastly reached Tom's house:

- Welcome! Welcome my dear good friend. Welcome to the house of mine. You've arrived only in period for lunch. Let us go! - beckoned, Tom.

- It smells scrumptious! I cannot wait to eat this particular food. - replied Milo that was starved.

- Help yourself, the friend of mine. There is cheese, milk, pasta, toast, peanut butter, fruit. and cake - stated Tom, proudly.

- Oh, wow! Thanks, I'm amazed with the lifestyle of yours. I believe I am going to stay right here with you.

The moment they started consuming, the servant on the house arrived. He entered the dining room as well as shooed the cats at bay with a stick:

- You filthy small creatures, get from here! That is not for you. Go eat anything you find outside.

The 2 friends ran out. Tom was very embarrassed:

- Do not worry, Milo. We are going to go back inside the moment he's gone. Today come with me, I am going to show you a place in which you can buy all kinds of food. - stated Tom, bravely.

- Wow! How's that? - directed Milo, amazed.

- It is a popular division store. - replied Tom

While the 2 cats wandered in the store, a male came towards them angrily using a broom.

- Run! Hurry up! Hide! - stated Tom out of breathing.

- Who's that? - Asked Milo, curiously. - My center is pounding.

- Don´t worry! That´s merely the owner of the shop. He does not like cats. Let us wait here for a couple of mins and wait till he vanishes entirely. Remain still. and quiet - whispered Tom.

- Oh, Tom, this's way too much for me. Before we had the servant with all the stick and so this male with a broom... - complained Milo.

- Well, do not exaggerate now. Just be cautious. - stated Tom, cooly.

- Well, appear here. I've had plenty of everything running about, jumping, perception frightened without being ready to consume in peace. This's not what I arrived for, therefore I think it will be my best interest to go back home on the countryside. It's very peaceful there. I miss it very much. - stated Milo, regrettably.

- I'm very sorry for those of this. - apologised, Tom.

- I prefer eating food that is fresh from the garden of mine than eating fancy meal in fear. I'd prefer to have an easy life as mine than a luxurious lifestyle like yours, wherever you can't enjoy something since you've to run and hide all the time. - stated Milo, sensibly.

In the conclusion Milo, abandoned the thought of living in a huge city. He packed the bag of his and went back to the beautiful house of his in the countryside in which he were living peacefully for the majority of his life.

The Story of The Little Marzipan Man

Once upon a period, there was a bit of small home where an old female used to live with the husband of her. They did not have kids and felt lonely. 1 day, the female decided to create a boy from marzipan. She got everything prepared then carefully started mixing all of the ingredients. After the dough was great, she rolled it wide open and eliminated the adorable little male's condition. The old female put the small marzipan male on a paper tray and then place the tray in the oven to bake.

After one hour, the existing female went to the oven and removed the tray. Since the small marzipan male was prepared, she added plenty of icing to create his mouth and hair. She used a bit of chocolate to make him eyes and some cherries to place several buttons on his belly.

After all that was done, the little marzipan man came alive. The old woman was shocked to see the little marzipan man running all around:

- Don't eat me – said the worried little marzipan man, as he jumped out of the window.

- Stop… Stop! Come back! – said the old woman, loudly.

- No one can catch me since I'm the little marzipan man- he stated as he ran as well as ran and ran.

The old woman, together with her husband, ran after him, but they couldn't catch him and the little marzipan man kept running and running.

While he was running, a sheep saw him:

- Hmm… you smell delicious. I'm going to eat you. – said the sheep looking at the little marzipan man.

- I just ran away from an old lady, which means I can run away from you too. I definitely can – said the little marzipan man, loudly while he laughed and ran all around.

T he sheep started chasing the little man, but the marzipan man was faster:

- Run, run as fast as you can, sheep. No one can catch me, since I'm the marzipan man. - mentioned the small male, bravely.

The sheep ran once him along with the old female, though none of them can capture him. The little marzipan male kept running, and quickly he satisfied a pig on path:

- You seem very yummy. I am gon na eat you right away. - mentioned the pig.

- You might consume me in case you might get me however, you can´t! - said the small marzipan man. - I ran far from a well used female, I ran away starting from a sheep and will try to escape from you. Run as quickly as you can, pig! Simply no business owner can get me since I'm the marzipan man. - mentioned the small male loudly as he ran.

The pig joined the used female and the sheep in chasing after the little marzipan male, but no even the pig can capture him.

The small marzipan male kept running and operating although he was operating a rabbit noticed him: - Hmm.... I believe I understand what I´ll have for lunch now. I could even feed the little ones of mine with this one. - stated the rabbit taking a look at the small marzipan male

- I ran far from an old lady, ran away from a sheep, ran at bay from a pig, and ran far from you, you little creature. Run, run as quickly as you can. Simply no business owner can get me since I'm the little marzipan male - said the small male, loudly, as he escaped from all of them.

The rabbit started running behind the little marzipan man and the rest of them but not even the agile rabbit could catch him.

The little marzipan man was very proud of himself. He kept running and running, till he saw a river in front of him. When he saw the river he slowed down. He was afraid the water would make him soggy.

There was a fox sipping water at the river.

- What a tasty meal for my stomach today – said the fox while looking at the little marzipan man – Hey, you ... little man, I think we should be friends. What do you think?

It was the first time the little marzipan man had ever heard anything like that and he was very pleased to hear it:

- My dear fox, I do not mind being your friend, but there is one condition – warned the little man.

- Go ahead, Mr. Marzipan – said the fox slowly.

- Could you please help me cross the river safely? – asked the little marzipan man, politely.

- Well, of course! – replied the fox – Why not, Mr. Marzipan man. Come, jump on my back. I will help you cross the river indeed.

The little marzipan man jumped on the fox's back and as soon as they reached the other side of the river, the fox quickly threw the up into the air with his nose, opened his big mouth, and went little marzipan man.

He was very tasty, indeed – said the fox with a smile and that was the end of the little marzipan man who lived a short yet adventurous life.

Stop Talking!

Ivan was sitting in the living room watching TV with his friends and whenever one of his friends started to talk Ivan talked too.

"Ivan, I was talking." His friend Eric said

"Yes, but I have something important to say," Ivan replied. Ivan always thought that what he had to say was more important than what others were saying

"We have important things to..." his friend Ed started to say as Ivan interrupted

"I think we should go outside" Ivan blurted out. Ed and Eric looked at one another and sighed.

Eric Asked, "and do what Ivan?"

"Oh let's..."Ed started to say

"Play football!" Ivan said

"I was going to say we could ride bikes but football is ok too," Ed whispered to Eri c

The boys began to play football. They played for about an hour and Ivan dropped the ball and said, "Ok now let's ride bikes."

The boys stopped and tried to tell Ivan they wanted to stop playing and just play cards, but Ivan kept interrupting. The boys finally went home for the night and Ivan was sitting with his Dad watching football on the TV.

"Didn't you and your friends…" Dad started to say

"I love football; we played in the yard today." Ivan piped up

"That is what I was going to ask you…"Dad tried to speak again

"I told them we needed to ride bikes" Ivan finished his comments.

"IVAN, stop interrupting me!" Dad said sternly, "did you enjoy playing with your friends? What did you talk about with them?" Dad finally finished a question

"Uhm, I think we talked about...." Ivan thought hard but couldn't remember anything they had talked about. "I don't remember what we talked about, that's weird"

"Ivan, you are a good friend but you like to interrupt..." Dad was making a good point but Ivan interrupte d

"I think I need to talk to the guys tomorrow and see what we talked about," Ivan said looking up at the ceiling

"Ivan, it's time for bed" Dad instructed.

The next morning came and Ivan saw Eric and Ed outside riding their bikes without him.

"Hey guys, what are you doing? You didn't' tell me you were going bike riding." Ivan questioned his friends.

"We were trying to tell you..."Ed started to talk

"I like riding bikes I can't believe you didn't come get me." Ivan interrupted again

"IVAN!" Ed yelled, "STOP TALKING!"

"Yeah Ivan, we have tried to tell you some things we want to do today but you kept interrupting us with just what you want to do and that's not fun for us all the time." Eric chimed in.

Ivan stood there looking confused. Had he interrupted so much that he didn't give his friends time to talk? Ivan walked back to his house and the guys rode off on their bikes

"Ivan why aren't you playing with Eric and Ed today," Dad aske d

"They didn't want to play with me today. They said I interrupted too much and they couldn't talk about what they wanted to do." Ivan shared

"Is there any truth to ……?" Dad said

"I just don't think I interrupt very much…." Ivan interrupted again. Dad stepped back and crossed his arms and looked at Ivan.

"You just interrupted me, Ivan," Dad said with a laugh

Ivan looked at the floor and then up at his dad. "I don't mean to. I just can't help keeping my thoughts in my head. They just pop out of my mouth." Ivan tried to explain

"Respecting other people's thoughts and ideas is important…." Dad started another sentence but Ivan started to talk

"I want my…" Ivan stopped himself. "I just did it again hu?"

"Yes, but at least you realized you did it and stopped." Dad encouraged him

The next day Ivan saw his friends again. "Hello Ed, hello Eric. What are you guys doing today?" Ivan asked

Ed looked at Eric, "We are…." Ed stopped talking expecting Ivan to interrupt. But he didn't so Ed continued, "We are going to go the pond and go fishing today. Would you like to join us?" Eric looked at Ed with a surprised look.

"Yes I would, thanks for inviting me," Ivan said with a happy voice. The boys headed to the pond to go fishing. The laughed and talked and no one interrupted.

"Ivan, we would have tried to invite you to go fishing the other day but you wouldn't let us talk so we just went with you. We are sorry but we are glad you came today we are having fun" Ed said with an excited voice

Ivan smiled and waited for Ed to finish then he said, "I am sorry I interrupted so much, I thought everyone just needed to hear what I wanted to say. But what I realized was that I missed out on what everyone else wanted to tell me and invite me to do. I think I have missed out on a lot because I interrupted so much."

The boys laughed and kept fishing until the sun started to go down. They had a good conversation where everyone got a chance to talk about what they wanted and the other boys could talk about it too and share their stories .

They sat on the bank of the pond with his friends enjoying their time together because he didn't interrupt and they all go to do something together that they all wanted to do.

Ivan got home after dinner and told his dad about the fun day he had that he tried hard to not interrupt. He shared that he learned a lot of new things about his friends that he didn't know before because he didn't interrupt.

"I'm proud of you Ivan. I know it is hard for you to wait your turn to talk but it sounds like you had a good day and that by waiting your turn your friends became better friends." Dad hugged Ivan "Waiting your turn to talk can help you learn new things so when you want to interrupt take a deep breath and wait your turn."

The Jaguar

"HaHa, that was funny!" Jenny Jaguar laughed.

Jenny thought everything was a joke and laughed at everything. Today Jenny thought the spilled juice on the kitchen floor was so funny. Her sister wasn't laughing and neither was her mom who was cleaning up the spilled juice.

"It's not all fun Jenny; your sister is very upset that she spilled her juice." Mom said .

Jenny ran upstairs to get her dolls and play in the living room. As she started to leave her room, she heard her mom coming up the stairs with the laundry basket of clean clothes. Jenny hid behind the door, covering her mouth so her mom couldn't hear her giggle. Her mom got closer and Jenny jumped out, "BOO!" Jenny yelled.

Mom got so startled that she threw the laundry basket in the air and all the clothes went flying everywhere. Jenny started laughing.

"Jenny this is not funny at all!" Mom said sternly "Now look at this mess, Jenny." Mom said looking around at the piles of clothes everywhere. Jenny giggled and ran down the stairs.

As Jenny played with her dolls in the living room, she noticed that the TV remote was sitting on the coffee table and she thought it would be funny to hide it from her Dad. She took the remote and put it under the cushion of her dad's favorite chair. She chuckled under breath. Her Dad came home from work and grabbed a glass of water and headed to the living room to watch the news. He sat in his favorite chair and reached for the remote…but it was not there. He looked around at the other tables, over the TV and under the newspaper on the coffee table.

"Hmmm that's odd," Dad said, "The remote is always in the same place, I wonder where it could be?" Jenny tried to hide her smile .

"Jenny, do you know where the remote is?" Dad Asked. Jenny shrugged her shoulders trying not to laugh out loud. "I always leave it on the coffee table." He continued.

Dad walked into the kitchen to ask mom if she knew where the remote was. Jenny waited until he left then put the remote back on the table then kept playing with her dolls. Dad came back into the room and stopped and looked at the remote with a confused look.

"Where did that come from?" Dad asked Jenny. Jenny fell back laughing

"I was joking, I hid it from you," Jenny picked up her dolls and left the living room

"That's not funny Jenny!" Dad called out to her as she left.

Jenny ran outside to play while she was still laughing.

Jenny caught up with her friends and they began to play hide and seek. It was a cool crisp Saturday morning in October and the leaves were all being raked up into huge piles. They were running around the piles hiding in the bushes and behind the trees. It was Jenny's turn to hide and she found the biggest pile of leaves in the neighbor's yard. She slipped behind the pile, moved a bunch of them around, and then laid on the ground and covered herself up to hide.

One of her friends saw her hide there and whispered to the other kids playing, "Jenny is in the leaves, she is always playing jokes on us so let's play one on her." The other kids agreed. They decided to hide in the other piles of leaves and wait to see if Jenny had jumped out to try to scare them.

Jenny waited and waited to be found but no one came. Just when she heard someone walking by. She waited until she thought they were right by her pile of leaves and then she popped up, "Surprise!" Jenny yelled. No one was there. No one was anywhere. Jenny looked around but she didn't see anyone. She walked around looking for the other kids that were hiding but didn't see anyone. She walked over by the tree house- nope.

She walked over by the swing sets in the back yard but no one was there either. Jenny started to get sad because she thought everyone had left her behind. She walked to the front yard and sat on the tire swing that hung in the big tree with a bunch of small piles of leaves on the ground.

"I just don't understand. Where did everyone go?" Jenny said with a sad voice .

Just then one by one the other kids started jumping out of the piles of leaves. "Jenny, we got you!" one of the kids yelled

"Ha Ha Jokes on you Jenny." Another one laughed

"That's not funny," Jenny said as she stood up crossing her arms

"Jenny you always play jokes on us so we decided to play on one on you. Come on it was funny." One of Jenny's good friends said. "If you don't like it maybe you shouldn't play so many jokes on us."

"My jokes don't hurt people's feelings," Jenny replied. But then Jenny thought about the spilled juice and how sad her sister was and remembered all the clean laundry her mom had to pick up because she jumped out and scared her. She started to think about how that could have made them feel. She stepped back from her friends and said that she needed to go but thanked them for hiding. She ran to her house and jumped in her dad's lap. "I'm sorry I made you miss your favorite show by hiding the remote." Jenny apologized. He kissed her on the head and then she ran off.

"Mom," Jenny yelled as she ran upstairs, "Mom, I'm sorry I made you spill all the clean clothes. It wasn't a funny joke. "

"Jenny, sometimes you are so funny but that was not nice. Thank you for apologizing." Mom said rubbing Jenny's hair.

Finally, Jenny went to her sister's room. "I know I didn't spill your juice but I laughed at you and I am sorry."

"It's ok but it made me sad." Her sister said, "I forgive you."

They both laughed and hugged and played dolls for the rest of the night.

Kendra the Kangaroo

Today was a big day for Kendra Kangaroo. It was her first day of 4th grade. She got up early and got ready to go before her mom was even out of bed.

"Kendra you are up early." Momma Kangaroo said when she came to the kitchen for coffee.

"I am so excited to go to 4th grade. I can't wait to see who is in my class and what new friends I will make." Kendra said stirring her cereal .

"You will do great honey, let me get ready to go and I'll drop you off," Momma replied as she took her coffee upstairs to get ready.

Kendra sat and thought about all the wonderful things that the 4th grade may bring. New friends, new teachers, new things to learn…her mind was running wild.

"Ok Kendra, Let's go!" Momma yelled. They hopped along the path to the school and talked about the fun Kendra was going to have.

"Remember though that the fence at the end of the schoolyard is as far as you can go. Don't jump that fence it is off-limits." Momma reminded Kendra as she kissed her head and sent her into the classroom

Kendra had a great first day. She met 3 new friends and loved her new teacher. Recess was such fun jumping rope and laughing. But one of the new students in her class, Reggy, was trying to get the other students to go out by the fence, that Momma Kangaroo warned Kendra about.

"No my Momma said that is off-limits," Kendra told Reggy. "That is outside of school grounds and we are not supposed to go there"

"Come on, what could happen?" Reggy said trying to coax them over the fence .

"I don't know but I'm not going!" Kendra said as she hopped back to class.

The next day came and Kendra met another new friend and learned some new math facts that she was good at. Then recess came again. Reggy ran out to the fence and stood up as high as he could to see what was on the other side. He was too short so he asked Kendra to hop up and see.

"I told you that area is off-limits," Kendra tried to remind him again.

Reggy stood up on the fence trying to look through the boards, "Kendra you are the only one who can jump over and see and then jump back. We need you to tell us what is over there."

Kendra shook her head no and went back to jump rope with the other students.

Kendra came home that day and asked her momma what was on the other side of the fence and why it was off-limits.

"Kendra that area is unsafe. There is a lot of construction work over there and it is not a place for children to play." Momma Kangaroo explained.

Kendra accepted that answer and didn't think about it again until Reggy brought it up at the next recess .

"Reggy, it's not safe over there. That's why there is a fence." Kendra told him

"It cannot be that bad. I think you are just afraid." Reggy taunted Kendra

"I am not afraid!" Kendra snapped back.

"Then jump the fence and jump back over. No one will ever know." Reggy stepped said and pointed over the fence.

Kendra stood there and remembered what her momma said but didn't want to be teased by the other students about being afraid. "How bad could one jump be?" She thought. If she jumped over and right back no one would be hurt and she could be back to class on time.

"FINE!" Kendra said. She jumped up and over the fence as the other students watched. She landed with a thump but yelled back to them. "Watch out I'm coming back over!"

Kendra jumped. She landed back on the same side. She jumped again but the ground was lower on that side of the fence and she couldn't jump that high.

"Hey, it's too high from this side," Kendra called out. Just then the recess bell rang and the kids ran back to class. Kendra kept trying to jump and jump but the fence was too high to get back over.

"Oh no, what am I going to do?" Kendra asked herself. She felt a tear coming to her eye because she knew she wasn't supposed to jump the fence but she didn't want to afraid either. What was she going to do?

Kendra started yelling over the fence and at the end of the day, someone finally responded.

"Kendra is that you?" the janitor called out

"YES! Please help me. I jumped the fence to show Reggy I could do it but it's too low over here and I can't get back over the fence." Kendra cried out.

"I will need to get help, Kendra. I will be right back." The Janitor replied. He came back with the teacher and Momma Kangaroo, who was very worried about her.

"I'm so sorry momma. I thought I could jump over it and get right back over but it's too low over here." Kendra said hanging her head.

"We will get you back on this side of the fence soon." Momma Kangaroo tried to reassure Kendra .

Kendra began to cry. She was embarrassed and disappointed that she didn't follow her directions and now so many people had come help her get out of the mess she was in.

"We need to remove some of the boards on the fence to get you back on this side of the fence. Stand back please." The Janitor told Kendra.

She stepped aside and heard the people on the other side start to remove the boards. One by one the boards were removed. It took several hours to remove what was needed. They removed a section big enough for

Kendra to hop back thru and once she hopped back thru everyone clapped.

"Kendra, do you know how much trouble you caused by not following directions?" Momma Kangaroo said. "We are glad you are safe but you had all of these people working extra hard to get you back into the schoolyard." Momma Kangaroo showed her all the people who had come to help rescue Kendra.

"I'm so sorry Momma, I knew better, I did. I didn't want Reggy to tell everyone I was afraid." Kendra tried to explain as she wrung her hands together and looked down at the ground.

"I understand, but there was a good reason you were not supposed to go over the fence and this is a good example of why you need to follow directions. None of you knew what was over there and you could have been hurt very badly." Momma Kangaroo hugged Kendra and told her that it was time to go home.

Kendra was relieved that she was rescued but felt bad because all those people came to help her because she didn't follow directions.

The next day she saw Reggy and told him what had happened and that she had to be rescued and that she didn't appreciate making her feel like she had to something against the rules.

Kendra didn't venture out by the fence or try to go where she was not supposed to again and she found that following directions was the easiest way to live each day.

Mother Duck

It was a bright summer time afternoon, mother duck found a lovely spot to lay the eggs of her; it was under a huge tree near a fish-pond. She laid 5 eggs. Suddenly she realised that one was completely different from the others. She was concerned because 4 of the eggs seemed normal, yellowish, and not overly large, while the unusual one was kind of gray and pretty large compared to the others. She made the decision never to consider it and waited for them to hatch.

One good morning, one after an additional, the eggs finally began to crack. All of the eggs had come in existence, and adorable little ducks have been poking their heads away into the world. All of the eggs cracked except one:

- Oh, examine my sweet babies - stated the mom duck, proudly - what a fortunate mum I'm ... I think about what happened on the fifth egg? It's taking such a very long time to hatch.

She sat on that particular egg and then gave to it all of the heat that she could:

- This can be the most incredible duck of all since it's taking so long to hatch; I'm certain of which - said mother duck full of hope One good morning, when the final egg broke, out arrived an ugly gentle yellow coloured duck. This duck was completely different from the additional ones; it was quite large, with hardly any feathers and a very strange colour:

- None of my additional ducks are like that; this method is very ... hideous - said the unhappy mother duck.

Mother duck hoped that 1 day, the ugly small duck would become just love the other babies of her. Days went by and also the ugly duck didn't change. All her brothers and sisters made entertaining of ugly duck and did not ever play with him. The ugly duck was extremely sad:

- You're not love us - believed one the child ducks - Look at which huge ugly thing - said a different one of the infants ducks - go away! You're very terrible to relax with us.

The ugly duck was truly sad since they have been all generating fun of him. Since nobody needed to relax with him, he began wandering around by yourself in the pond and looked at his reflection in the water:

- No one desires to relax with me. Why am I very ugly? - cried the little bit duck

The ugly duck could not stop thinking about the text that the brothers of his and sisters had mentioned to him. He began crying and as he stopped he chose to leave the family of his.

The unsightly duck wandered all on your own away from the pond which used to be the home of his. Soon when winter arrived, there's ice all around and also the ugly duck received depressing. He started out shivering due to the cold. He couldn't find some foods to eat or maybe some warm spot to stay. He watched a family of ducks and also went to them, though they rejected him due to the looks of his.

Then he went towards the hen's house, but all of the small hens began pecking at him with the beaks of theirs, therefore he didn't have other option besides try to escape.

While wandering, he satisfied a dog but if the dog noticed just how terrible the duck was, he scampered away:

- I'm so ugly that possibly even the hunting dog wants absolutely nothing to do with me - whined the duck Discouraged, the unsightly duck began wandering about once again, as he satisfied a farmer, whom has taken him home to his children and wife. Regrettably, maybe even in the peasant's home, he was troubled by the cat which existed there, therefore he left.

Quickly it was springtime and everything was green and fresh once again. Suddenly the unsightly duck saw a river just where he watched a lovely swan swimming. He fell for her, though the ugly duck was extremely ashamed of himself, therefore he bowed. When he bent his head, he saw the reflection of his in warm water and was astonished. He was not ugly anymore.

He'd transformed right into a lovely young swan. He realised the reason he looked completely different from the siblings of his; he would have been a swan and were ducks!

He married the beautiful swan he'd fallen in love with and were living happily ever after.

The OX

Once upon a period, there would have been a pond wherein a group of frogs utilized to live, collectively, gladly. They spent their days playing and helping one another do everything. Nevertheless, they weren't all the same; there is one known as Kermit who was probably the skinniest of all of them. She might jump to the pinnacle of every stone. Yet another one was, Wart. He was the quickest of them all; he might get flies before anybody else may see them. There was, too, Ribbit that was the biggest of all of them.

Every day, Ribbit had more than a dozen flies and insects for lunch and dinner. The other frogs were scared of him because of his huge size. Ribbit loved to get attention and felt proud of his size. He quite often used to make fun of the smaller frogs:

- Haha. Could you leap onto the top stone? Does that mean you can get away from larger animals that would like to attack you? Very well, great for you - stated Ribbit, sarcastically - I do not require that ability, because no one is as large as I'm.

- Do you think that nobody is as big as you are, Ribbit? – asked Kermit, curiously.

- How do we know that? We've never seen a bigger frog than him – wondered Wart.

All the frogs of the pond thought Ribbit was the biggest animal on the planet; they weren't used to seeing other frogs or animals since the pond was deep in the forest. Ribbit liked to believe that too. He had four babies who played with the other frogs near the pond:

- Hey! Let's go and play beyond that tree. There are so many big stones over there. – suggested one of Ribbit's babies.

- Oh, I would rather not go there. My mommy told me to play on this side of the pond and I do not want to disobey. – said another shy frog.

- Oh, come on! My daddy is the biggest animal on the planet; if any trouble comes along, we'll just call him. Don't worry, my little friend. – replied Ribbit's baby.

- Hmm, I don't know. My mum will be really mad at me if she finds out – said the shy frog.

- Oh, come on! Don't worry! If she says anything, we´ll just ask my daddy to talk to her. Come with us. – said Ribbit's babies , altogether.

- Hmm, ok then. You convinced me. Let's go! - said the shy but eager frog.

Without wasting a single second, all the small frogs hopped and jumped to the other side of the pond beyond the big tree. They were surprised to see that there was another small pond right under the big tree:

- Oh, look at that! There is another pond here! I thought there was just one pond on the entire planet. – said one of the frogs.

- Oh, what are you saying? There are so many things that we haven't seen yet. Our planet is quite huge. – said another of Ribbit's babies.

- Enough with the talking, let's play now! – said yet another from the group.

All the frogs leaped onto the highest stone and then, one after another, they jumped into the pond. Suddenly the ground started shaking:

- Oh! No! What is happening now? Why is everything moving? – said Ribbit's babies full of freight.

- I knew it! I should have listened to my mummy. We never should have left the pond! We are all going to die! – said the shy frog

Suddenly a strange looking creature appeared walking towards the pond. It was as tall as the highest stone. It´s belly wiggled with every step it took and it made a loud noise. When the frogs saw him, they got scared and leapt onto the stones as fast as they could to get away. Unfortunately, one of them slipped and fell into the pond:

- What is going on here? Who are you, little creatures? I've never seen you before! – said a very big and curious ox.

- Oh! Please! Don´t eat me. I beg you. – said the fallen frog.

- What? Eat you? Ha, ha, ha .... Why on earth would I want to eat a small creature like you? I am here, just because I am thirsty and I want to drink some water. – said the ox, amused by the frogs musings.

- Oh! Does that mean you will not attack us? – asked the fallen frog.

- No, no. I do not eat frogs! – replied the ox, matter of factly.

- Then, what do you eat? How did you get so big? ... My daddy eats tons of insects in a day and he is not even half your size. – said one of Ribbit's babies from behind a stone.

- Your daddy? Do you mean a frog? Ha, ha, ha ... A frog can never be as big as I am, even if it eats all the insects on the planet. I was born this size. Every animal has its size. – replied the ox, wisely.

- You mean other animals are bigger than you? – asked one of the frogs from the group.

- Of course! – replied the ox.

The group of little frogs was surprised to hear about other animals being even bigger than the ox itself. They sat there for many hours listening to the fascinating stories, the ox informed them, about some other animals.

As shortly as nighttime fell, the number of small frogs said goodbye to the new friend of theirs.

- We need to go home! Hurry up! I cannot wait to express to these accounts to daddy. - claimed one of Rabbit's babies.

- Yes! Let's go! – agreed the other frogs.

When the little frogs arrived home, they went straight to Ribbit and told him the entire tale. The stories were so amusing that all the other frogs of the pond gathered to listen:

- Ha, ha, ha! …. My babies, you are so naive! Did you just say that this Mr. Ox was bigger than me? – asked Ribbit.

- Not just that, daddy! – replied one of Ribbit's babies. - He said that other animals are even bigger than him. They go to the pond over there to drink water. He also said that you can never be as big as he is.

- Well! That's crazy! How can anybody be as big as I am? He misled you. He must have bloated himself up just to appear bigger than me. This Mr. Ox is a big liar. – said Ribbit, angrily.

- Well, Ribbit, what Mr. Ox said can be true. I always talk to the birds that come to drink water here in our pond. I have heard stories about other animals from them. It would be a big mistake to think that we are the greatest. – said one of the frogs, wisely.

- It is your mistake, not mine! I am the biggest creature on this planet! That is a fact! – said Ribbit, arrogantly.

- I have an idea. Why don't we wait until tomorrow morning? We can go together to the other pond and find out. The little frogs said that these huge animals go there to drink water. We will go there in the morning, hide behind a stone and find out the truth. – suggested another wise frog.

All the frogs there approved the idea, except Ribbit, who was furious. He had to prove that he was the biggest of them all; otherwise, he was afraid no one would ever respect him again:

- No! We have to decide this right now! Nobody will fool me or my babies. Mr. Ox thought that he could get away with his lies. How dare he say that I can never be as big as he is? – shouted Ribbit, angrily.

Ribbit stretched his back and stood straight, and then he bloated his stomach to be even bigger:

- Now, tell me. Was he as big as this? – asked Ribbit.

- No, daddy! He was much bigger than that. – replied one of Ribbit's sons.

- Was he as big as this? – asked Ribbit while bloating his stomach a tad more.

- No! He was way bigger than that... Stop it! Don't do that! Every animal has different skills and sizes. I am pretty sure Mr. Ox can't jump the way we do. – said another very wise frog from the group.

- Yes, daddy, you have to stop bloating up like that or you'll burst. – said a very worried frog.

Ribbit was not ready to give up, he did not want to listen to what the others had to say. All he could think about were these words " As big as an ox, as big as an ox, as big as an ox..." He ignored everyone and bloated his stomach up even more than before:

- Was he as big as this? – asked Ribbit out of breath.

- No, daddy! He was so much bigger than that. – replied his honest babies.

- What about this; was he as big as this? - asked Ribbit arching his back.

- No, daddy! He was a million times bigger than that. – said his babies.

- What about this? What about this? – asked Ribbit while his stomach grew and his face was turned blue.

- Ribbit, please, stop it! Can't you see that you are hurting yourself? – said one of the wisest frogs.

That frog was right. Ribbit was hurting himself. His back was stretched out, his eyes popped out of his face and his stomach was so blown up it was aching but he refused to give up. He wanted to prove that he was the biggest animal of all. He took a deep breath and then ... popped. Unfortunately, Ribbit had gone beyond his limit.

- Oh, Ribbit - all the frogs cried - If only you had listened! We are all big in our way. There is no need to compare yourself to any other animal.

Quin

"Want to hear a story?" Quin asked the other quails pecking at the ground for grubs. "I have a good one".

They all looked at each other and agreed a good story was fun to listen to. So they nestled down into the grass to listen to what Quin had to say.

"One day while I was walking along the river bank, I saw a fish sitting on a rock..." the other quails looked at one another in disbelief, "....He was eating a worm sandwich and enjoying the afternoon. I walked up to him and asked if he wanted to share his worm sandwich and he gave me half of it."

"This is not a true story Quin, fish don't sit on rocks eating worm sandwiches," another Quail said from the group.

"Well it's my story," Quin replied and continued "We sat together eating the delicious worm sandwich and talking about how the trees were starting to turn orange for the fall."

The other quails laughed and started to leave, "This is a good story Quin, and fish can't talk. "

Quin thought the story was a good one and could be believable to someone. He walked away and pecked at the ground some more.

A few days later Quin asked, "Want to hear a story? I have a good one." A couple of the quail agreed and settled into the grass to listen.

"The other day I was splashing around in the puddles and a bobcat came over to me asking me for directions...." Quin started to tell his tale

"Wait a minute, a bobcat? That would want to have you for lunch not ask you for directions" one of the quails squeaked.

"It's my story I can tell it however I want," Quin replied

"Well, it's not very believable." One quail said as she walked away.

Quin was getting frustrated that no one wanted to listen to his stories. They were stories after all so they didn't need to be believable. Quin stopped asking if they wanted to hear his stories and he began writing them down. He made a whole bunch of stories. He took the stories to the place where the books were made for people to read and they took his stories and made a whole book of them. He signed the stories as Q. INN and took the books back to where all the other Quails were.

"Look at this great book I found!" Quin started passing out the books.

The other quails began reading the stories and talking about them. They read stories all day. Some stories were funny.... some were sad and some were very serious but they all loved the stories. They wondered who this Q. INN was.

"He must be a genius." One Quail said

"A Mastermind at writing." Another chimed in

"I wonder if he will write more?" a third Quail said .

Quin was so excited to see everyone enjoying his stories that he began to write more and put another book together. The other quails couldn't wait to get their hands on it and read the Q. INN stories.

A few weeks later Quin thought he would try to tell one of the stories he wrote.

"Want to hear a story?" Quin asked the other quails. "I have a good one"

"No, we are enjoying reading the stories of Q. INN. They are great!" the quails all said and agreed.

Quin was discouraged but happy at the same time. They loved his stories in the book but didn't want to hear him tell the stories. He decided that was ok after all they were still his stories.

The place that makes the books was selling out of the books very fast and they asked Quin to write one more book of stories for them and he agreed. But this time they wanted him to go to the store and talk about his books to everyone who loved them so much. Quin thought about it and wondered if all the quails knew it was him writing would they still like the books? They didn't want to hear him tell the stories but they wanted to read about them. Quin agreed to one more book and he set out to put it together. A few weeks passed and the book was ready to go .

The bookmaker put out signs advertising that Q. INN would be coming to talk about the books himself and everyone was so excited.

"Maybe Q. INN will sign my book," One quail asked

"I want my picture taken with him" Another added

The day came and it was time to put out the new book. Quails were lined up all across the yard waiting for the new book from Q. INN. When the time came the bookmaker stepped out on the stage.

"We are excited to present this newest book of stories from Q. INN. Today we have a special guest here to talk to you, sign your books and if you want, he will even take a photo with you" the Bookmaker said with excitement. Everyone cheered and waited in anticipation for Q. INN to come out.

When Quin came out from behind the curtain, the quails were very surprised. They didn't know that Quin and Q. INN were the same person. They applauded and pushed their way up to the stage to hear more stories.

Quin began telling more stories and they all listened very closely. When Quin was done, they all lined up to talk to him and tell him what a great storyteller he was and they just didn't give him a chance before but they were glad he didn't give up what he liked to do because they enjoyed this books and stories more than ever.

Quin felt good about writing the books and that he kept doing what he liked even if they didn't listen to him at first. Now he could tell stories and everyone would listen. It felt good to do what he loved to do.

The Red Fox

Reggie Red Fox was going on vacation. He was so excited that he packed his bags a week early. He had made all his travel plans months in advance so he was sure to know exactly what he was going to do.

The day came and he went off on his vacation. He traveled very far and saw some amazing things along the way there. Once he reached his vacation spot, he got all settled into his room and began to unpack. He sat down at the desk and looked over the stuff he was planning to do. He had planned so many things that he was not sure he would be able to do them all. He rethought his schedule and decided it could work if he hurried through some of the things he planned.

He went to bed early and dreamed of the fun things he was going to do the next day. Even in his dream, he had to hurry through the places he was so excited to see. So when he woke up, he felt confident that he could see everything right on schedule.

First stop was the historic battleground where his great grandfather fought some battles. Reggie though the battlefield was very interesting, but he had to run by all the things to look at to get to the next activity.

Next Stop-Candy Factory. Reggie wanted to visit here because he loved candy and wanted to see how they made it. He walked into the factory and started walking along the glass wall to see the candy being made. He enjoyed the part where all the candy got dipped into the chocolate and rolled out to get wrapped up. He stood watching and could watch this for hours. But... Beep bee beep. His alarm went off alerting him it was time to go to the next adventure.

He jumped on the bus and whisked away to the park for a music concert by one of his favorite bands. He arrived at the park and got ready for the concert to start but couldn't stop thinking about the candy factory and all the yummy goodness he had to leave behind. He was in such a hurry he didn't even get to buy any to take with him.

"Oh well, next time," he thought to himself. Then the concert started. The music was wonderful; everyone was dancing and singing along. Then Beep Bee beep...the alarm sounded again. Reggie grabbed his bag and headed out of the park. Just as he was leaving, he heard the band start to play his most favorite song. He stopped for a moment and wondered if he should stay just for one more song. If he stayed, he would miss the train to the next stop. He hurried off and got on the train.

"It sure would have been nice to have some fresh candy while I was listening to my favorite song at the park. I am so busy I am missing out on the best parts of what I wanted to do." Reggie thought again to himself, "What if just come back another time and do them again, so I can get what I missed. It will be ok, think of all the things I will still get to do today" he resolved himself to keep going.

The train pulled to the station and Reggie got off and headed to the museum. This was a museum about dinosaurs and Reggie loved dinosaurs. He walked in the door and was overwhelmed with all the amazing statues of the dinosaurs. There was the Brontosaurus, the Stegosaurus, the T-Rex and the Triceratops- His favorite. This was a wonderful place. All of the dinosaur fossils and Beep bee beep- time to leave the museum. All this leaving was getting tiresome and he was not able to see everything he wanted to see. Maybe he planned to do too much stuff. "Wasn't the purpose of a vacation to relax?" He thought.

He decided to not go to the next planned event and instead stay at the museum and keep looking at the Dinosaurs. As he made his way through the displays, he came across a room in the museum playing a movie about dinosaurs. He sat and watched it for a long time.

"This is a great movie." Said one of the spectator.

"Yes, it is and when this will be over we get to go out in the back and dig up dinosaur bones." The other person said.

"What! I didn't know that was part of the museum activity! This is GREAT!" Reggie sad excitedly

After the move finished everyone went outside and they received a small brush and a shovel so they could dig up some fossil bones and dust them off. Reggie took his stuff and went right to work. He was moving dirt and rocks around and then he paused. Was it, could it be? A dinosaur bone right in front of him. Reggie began to move the dirt away and used the brush to dust off the bone.

"I found one!" Reggie yelled .

Everyone came rushing over to watch and see what Reggie had found. Reggie finished moving the dirt away and gently picked up the bone and held it up for everyone to see. Everyone was very excited. The lady in charge of the dig called Reggie over to the table to inspect the bone and let him know what kind of dinosaur it came from.

Reggie placed the bone on the table and she measured it and put it on the scale to see how much it weighed. She looked at with a special pair of glasses and then looked at Reggie.

"Well, you have found the bone of a Triceratops." She said with a smile

"That's my favorite dinosaur." Reggie shrieked "Can I keep it?" He asked

"No, we need to keep it here and see if we can find the rest of the dinosaur that this bone belongs to." The lady said.

Reggie wasn't sad about not being able to keep the bone. He was excited that he found it. He thought about how he could have missed out on this whole part of the trip if would have stuck to his plan and left the museum. He was glad he slowed down to enjoy his vacation.

Noel the Newt Sings Too Loud

"Good afternoon class. My name is Mr. Melon and I am going to be your music teacher this year. I'm looking forward to all of your singing voices making gorgeous music." Mr. Melon launched himself on the second - grade choir class.

"Today we are going to sing some songs we all know so it's easy to learn how we all sound and sing together." Mr. Melon continued.

The class began to sing and then one person began to yell out louder than everyone else. Noel was singing louder than everyone else. Mr. Melon didn't say anything as he was just learning how everyone sang and thought maybe Noel was just joking around.

The next day came and they began to practice again. Noel sang louder again and Mr. Melon tried to direct him to sing with the class but it didn't work.

After class, Mr. Melon called Noel over to ask him why he sang so loud.

"I can't hear myself if I sing like everyone else so I sing louder so I can hear myself singing," Noel said confidently and walked out of the class.

His explanation seemed to make sense but how was Mr. Melon going to teach Noel that singing as a group would help everyone be heard equally.

The next day the class took turns singing solo songs and Noel sung his song wonderfully. Mr. Melon was sure he could have Noel sing more but he still needed to teach him how to sing with the group when needed.

The choir started to prepare for the upcoming spring concert and they began learning new songs none of them had ever sung before. This meant that they needed to learn how to sing the songs as a group. The groups sounded so good together but when Noel learned the words by heart, he began singing over everyone else again.

Mr. Melon was so confused and he thought about it for a long time. He decided to have the class listen some other famous groups of singers and show the class that if everyone sang together, they could sound just like those groups.

The next day he played music from many different music groups and other choirs. He explained that they sounded so good because everyone sang together as a group and the only time anyone sang out was when they sang a solo .

Noel heard this and wondered how all those other people could hear themselves to know if they were singing well or not. Noel stayed after class to talk to Mr. Melon about that. "How do you know if you are singing well if you can't hear yourself?"

"Noel, a choir is a group of people who sing together to show how well they can work together to sing a song. Not one person's voice is above another. The beauty of a choir is that they all have harmony and when they all sing together the sound can be very pleasant." Mr. Melon tried to explain

"I am not very big," Noel tried to explain. "Are you sure that I shouldn't sing louder so we can make sure I am singing the song, right?"

Mr. Melon smiled and said, "Let's try tomorrow to sing with the class and see if we can make the song sound better than ever."

Noel sang all the way home in a quieter voice to see if he still sounded good. "Not bad." He said to himself.

The next day the choir sang together and they sounded magnificent. All the voiced were melting together and sounded perfect. Everyone was heard equally and it made the song the best they had ever sung .

"Noel, Great job today! You sounded GREAT!" Mr. Melon encouraged us at the end of class.

The class arrived at the spring concert and stood ready to deliver the performance they had been practicing for. The music began and they began singing. Noel was having a tough time hearing himself once again and thought if he might simply sing louder though he remembered what Mr. Melon had declared with each other they created the very best audio so Noel sang his very best with the choir.

After the performance, everyone stood upwards as well as cheered for them. What a moment with the choir. A standing ovation. Mr. Melon stood proudly alongside the class of his and urged them to bow. The pupils exited the point and waited for the majority of the concert to be over. Mr. Melon entered the kitchen with the hands of his behind the back of his.

What do you've behind your back? one of several pupils asked.

Something really valuable. Something which I think you'll all like. Mr. Melon stated since he pulled an azure ribbon out originating from turning the rear of his. Many of the pupils gasped as well as cheered.

"Have we won the blue ribbon?" they all asked .

"We did indeed. We showed the judges that we could work as a team and sing together and they thought we did the best job over everyone." Mr. Melon proudly exclaimed.

After all the students went up to see the Blue Ribbon, Noel stepped up to the ribbon.

"We won this because they could hear us all? They thought we sounded the best?" Noel Asked

"That is correct Noel. We sang together as a group and they thought we sounded the best. I am so proud of you for trying hard to sing with the group. Because of everyone's hard work and your effort to sing quieter we won this prize." Mr. Melon shared holding up the ribbon again.

"I'm glad I learned to work and sing as part of the choir and not sing loud. I actually can hear myself when we sing together and I can see how when we work together, great things happen." Noel smiled and said as he gave Mr. Melon a high five.

The Paper Airplane

Have you ever been on an airplane ride before?

You sit down in a seat, you buckle yourself in, and when the pilot turns on the engine, you pick up speed down the runway until you are heading up, and up, and up into the sky, all the way to the clouds.

Flying can be fun, and even if you have never been on an actual airplane before, you can imagine it in your mind.

You can fly wherever you want to go on your very own airplane, and tonight, as you draw the covers up over you and snuggle into bed, you can fly to your dreams on your paper airplane.

Have you ever made a paper airplane before?

It's so easy and fun, and with just a few folds on a sheet of paper, you can make a flying machine.

Let's try to imagine it now.

Close your eyes and take a deep breath and let it out.

Imagine a blank piece of paper in your mind.

Can you see it?

If you need a real piece of paper first to make an airplane, that's okay too.

Try just to imagine it in your mind if you can.

The piece of paper may be flat right now, but as soon as you fold it in new ways, it will become something else, something special .

In your imagination, fold your paper to become a paper airplane…

Fold it in half longways first…

Open it back up and fold the corners down at the top to make the plane's point…

Now, you can fold it in half again, longways, so that your plane has a point…

Next, you fold the sides down to make the wings.

Remember?

Piece of cake, with just a few folds in your imagination, you have yourself a paper airplane.

Now, can you imagine it flying in your mind?

Imagine holding it in your hand and launching it across your bedroom.

Where does it fly?

Your paper airplane will take you on a journey tonight, a great adventure around the world so you can see lots of new places and people and feel relaxed through your creative imagination.

All you have to do is take a deep breath and imagine yourself becoming the size of the airplane, or perhaps the paper airplane grows larger to match your size.

You can climb aboard your paper airplane and become the pilot!

Put your goggles on and strap on your flying cap.

Start your engines and get ready to take off into the starry night sky.

You can fly out of your bedroom window or take off from the roof of your house.

Use your imagination to help you get off the ground and flying in your plane...

You can see your neighborhood as you fly over the house.

Perhaps you see a few friends from school looking out of their bedroom windows now, wondering how on earth you managed to get your flying, paper airplane.

Your neighborhood is flying past you as your plane picks up speed and gets slightly higher in the sky.

You can go fly all over the world tonight and see some wonderful places.

Where would you like to go first?

The Pyramids in Egypt would be an amazing adventure...

Let's go there!

Your paper airplane knows just where to go.

You fly over the land until you reach the ocean, and you see how big the world is.

There are so many giant continents and countries to visit.

From your view on the plane, you can look down on the world like a map like you have seen in geography books.

The map of the world shows all of the places you can visit.

You see the landmass of Africa, and your airplane flies toward it.

You can almost see the top of the pyramids from your plane as you fly closer to Egypt.

There they are!

You can see them so clearly, these giant human-made sculptures, these ancient and beautiful tombs!

Your plane flies around the tops of the pyramids, doing loop-de-loops, enjoying the beautiful view from the plane.

All around the pyramids, you can see the sand that is warmed by the sun.

It is a hot, dry land, and it feels soothing in the sun as you fly over the ancient pyramids.

Now, you are ready to see more.

Where to next in your paper airplane?

Let's go to the Amazon Rainforest!

Your airplane swirls around and heads back across the ocean and over to South America, where a whole other culture of life has thrived for millennia.

You can see from high up in your paper airplane the thick forest of trees that cover much of the continent's upper part.

You can see the Amazon River, the largest river in the world, flowing and branching off throughout the jungle of life below.

The jungle is thick and steamy and full of many sounds.

Your paper airplane flies lower, down to the treetops and into the forest so that you are flying under the canopy of trees.

Inside the forest, the plane takes you safely through the jungle, swerving through plants and vines and fruits and flowers.

Colorful birds are cawing and singing.

Monkeys are hanging from the trees and bellowing and hooting hellos to you as you fly by.

Long, large, silent, colorful snakes are dripping off of tree branches.

Colorful frogs talk to each other on the trees while Macaws flap their wings and fly through the jungle.

A jaguar runs and bounds, keeping pace with your plane as you fly through and up and out of the canopy of trees.

What a magnificent place to see!

Where to next in your paper airplane?

To the romantic city of Paris, France, perhaps?

Your plane swirls around and loop-de-loops back across the great, big Atlantic Ocean over Africa and Morocco and into France's country.

You can nearly see the Eiffel Tower from your plane; it is that striking and obvious to your eyes.

Your plane swirls closer to the tower and flies around it, from the bottom to the top.

There are people everywhere in the city, walking to and from, sipping beverages, talking, and laughing.

Your airplane flies over the river Seine following it like a roadway.

You can see men and women kissing and dancing.

You can hear the romantic sound of accordion music playing all over the city.

You can smell the delicious foods and pastries and desserts coming out fresh and enjoyed by Parisian people at the cafés on the sidewalk.

Ah, Paris. The city of love.

Your plane is whisking you off again and taking you across Europe, all the way over to China.

The Great Wall of China is huge and long and was built many centuries ago.

It is a sight to see, and your paper airplane is taking you on a journey along the great wall.

You can see how big China is from up in the air.

It stretches far and wide.

You fly over men and women in the rice fields, harvesting one of their most important foods.

You see, Panda Bears munching on bamboo in thick bamboo forests.

Your plane flies a little closer for a better look at these beautiful creatures.

They are snuggled together eating all day long.

Now, you are ready for one more trip before heading home on your plane.

You fly to a little island off the coast of America called Hawaii.

You can see from your paper airplane the tropical flowers, plants, and trees that cover the island.

You can see a volcano steaming on the horizon, and your plane swirls around the smoke coming out of the top .

You can hear the drumming on the beach at night here.

The people are having a luau, dancing to the drums in front of the firelight, next to the ocean waves.

Your plane flies over the party.

You feel so happy to see such a vibrant scene of people celebrating.

It is the perfect time for you to fly back home in your paper airplane.

You fly across the sea, to wherever your home may be.

You find your way back to your neighborhood, flying past all of the house s of people you know, wishing them sweet dreams as you fly overhead.

Your plane can fly through your bedroom window and become as small as a piece of paper again.

You are here in your room, and your paper airplane is beside you.

Your room is safe and cozy and warm.

You are surrounded by love and comfort.

You can fall fast asleep now that you have been far and wide in your paper airplane.

It has taken you on a great and wonderful journey around the world, and now it is time for a good night's rest.

Your plane will carry you into your dreams tonight.

Where would you like to go?

Take your plane to any place you would like as you drift off into your dreamworld.

You can fly across the globe; you can land your plane anywhere you like.

Imagine yourself on a great journey of discovery as you fall fast asleep.

Your dreams will carry you farther than you have ever been before.

May your journey be exotic, exciting, and fun.

Tomorrow will be another great adventure.

Sleep tight!

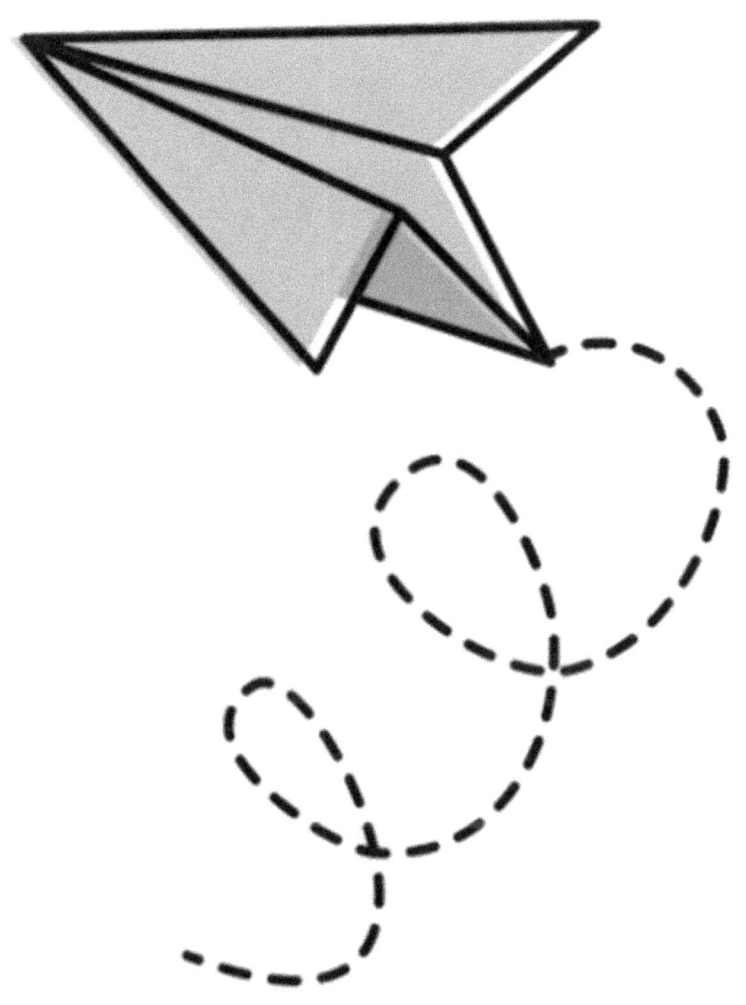

www.ingramcontent.com/pod-product-compliance
Lightning Source LLC
Chambersburg PA
CBHW070933080526
44589CB00013B/1496